REPORT

OF

MR. WOOD'S VISIT

TO THE

CHOCTAW AND CHEROKEE MISSIONS.

1855.

BOSTON:
PRESS OF T. R. MARVIN, 42 CONGRESS STREET.
1855.

REPORT.

At the meeting of the Board held in Utica, New York, September, 1855, the Prudential Committee submitted a special communication in reference to the Choctaw and Cherokee missions, in which they say: "Since the last meeting of the Board, it has seemed desirable that one of the Secretaries should visit the Indian missions in the South West, for the purpose of conferring fully and freely with them in reference to certain questions which have an important bearing upon their work. Mr. Wood, therefore, was directed to perform this service; which he did in the spring of the present year. After his return to New York, he drew up a report of this visit, and presented the same to the Prudential Committee. It is deemed proper that this document should be laid before the Board at the earliest opportunity; and it is herewith submitted. The results obtained by this conference are highly satisfactory to the Committee."

The report of Mr. Wood is in the following language:

To the Prudential Committee of the American Board of Commissioners for Foreign Missions:

I have to report a visit made by me to the Choctaw and Cherokee missions, in obedience to instructions contained in the following resolutions adopted by you, March 6, 1855:

"*Resolved*, 1. That Mr. Wood be requested to repair to the Choctaw Nation, at his earliest convenience, with a view to a fraternal conference with the brethren in that field in respect to the difficulties and embarrassments which have grown out of the action of the Choctaw Council in the matter of the boarding schools, and also in respect to any other question which may seem to require his attention.

"2. That, in case the spring meeting of the Choctaw mission shall not occur at a convenient time, he be authorized to call a meeting at such time and place as he shall designate.

"3. That on his return from the Choctaw mission he be requested to confer with the brethren of the Cherokee mission, in regard to any matter that may appear to call for his consideration, and that he be authorized to call a meeting for this purpose.

"4. That on arriving in New York he be instructed to prepare a report, suggesting such plans and measures for the adoption of the Committee in reference to either of these missions as he may be able to recommend."

Leaving New York, March 19, and proceeding by the way of the Ohio and Mississippi rivers to Napoleon, thence up the White river, across to Little Rock, and through Arkansas to the Choctaw country, I arrived at Stockbridge, April 11. Including the portions of the days occupied in passing from one station to another, I devoted three days to Stockbridge, three to Wheelock, six to Pine Ridge, three to Good-water, and three to Spencer; the latter a station of the mission of the General Assembly's Board. Five days, with a call of a night and half a day at Lenox, were occupied in the journey to the Cherokee country, in which I spent two days at Dwight, and three at Park Hill; my departure from which was on the 11th of May, just one month from my arrival at Stockbridge. My return to New York was on May 31, ten and a half weeks from the time of leaving it.

I should do injustice to my own feelings, and to the members of the two missions, not to state that my reception was everywhere one of the utmost cordiality. The Choctaw mission, when my coming was announced, agreed to observe a daily concert of prayer that it might be blessed to them and the end for which they were informed it was designed. They met me in the spirit of prayer; our intercourse was much a fellowship in prayer; and, through the favor of Him who heareth prayer, its issue was one of mutual congratulation and thanksgiving.

The visit, although a short one, afforded considerable opportunity (which was diligently improved) for acquainting myself with the views, feelings, plans and labors of the brethren of the missions. Their attachment to their work, and to the Board with which they are connected, is unwavering. With fidelity they prosecute the great object of their high calling; and in view of the spiritual and temporal transformation taking place around them, as the result of the faithful proclamation of the gospel, we are compelled to exclaim, "What hath God wrought!" It was pleasant to meet them, as with frankness and fraternal affection they did me, in consultation for the removal of difficulties, and the adoption of measures for the advancement of the one end desired equally by them and by the Prudential Committee.

Several topics became subjects of conference, on some of which action was taken by the missions; and on others recommendations will be made by the Deputation, that need not be embraced in this report. In respect to them all, there was entire harmony between the Deputation and the missions.

In their first resolution, the Committee requested me to repair to the Choctaw Nation, with special reference to the embarrassments and difficulties which have grown out of the action of the Choctaw Council in the matter of the boarding schools. A condensed statement of the action of the Council, and of the missionaries and Prudential Committee, previous to the sending of the Deputation, seems to be here called for.

In the year 1842, the Choctaw Council, by law, placed four female seminaries "under the direction and management of the American Board of Commissioners for Foreign Missions," subject only to "the conditions, limitations, and restrictions rendered in the act." In accordance with the act, a contract was entered into, by which the schools were taken for a period of twenty years. The "conditions, limitations and restrictions" specified in the act and contract, so far as they bind the Board, are the following: 1. The superintendents and teachers, with their families, shall board at the same table with the pupils. 2. In addition to letters, the pupils shall be taught housewifery and sewing. 3. One-tenth of the pupils are to be orphans, should so many apply for admission. 4. The Board shall appropriate to the schools a sum equal to one-sixth of the moneys appropriated by the Choctaw Council. With these exceptions, the "direction and management" of the schools were to be as exclusively with the Board, as of any schools supported by the funds of the Board.

Thus the schools were carried forward until 1853. At the meeting of the Council in that year, a new school law, containing several provisions, (and sometimes spoken of in the plural as "laws,") was enacted, bringing the Board, through its agents, under new "conditions, restrictions and limitations." A Board of Trustees was established, and a General Superintendent of schools provided for, to discharge various specified duties, for the faithful performance of which they are to give bonds in the sum of $5,000. The enactments of this law, affecting the agents of the Board under the existing contract, are the following:

1. The Board of Trustees, convened by the General Superintendent, are to hear and determine difficulties between a trustee and any one connected with the schools; to judge of the fitness of teachers, etc., and request the Missionary Boards to remove any whose removal they may think called for; and, in case of neglect to comply with their wishes, to report the same to the Commissioner of Indian Affairs through the United States Agent. Section 5.

2. The Trustees are to select the scholars from their several districts. Section 7.

3. No slave or child of a slave is to be taught to read or write "*in* or *at* any school," etc., by any one connected in any capacity therewith, on pain of dismissal and expulsion from the nation. Section 8.

4. Annual examinations are to take place at times designated by the General Superintendent. Section 10.

5. The Trustees are empowered to suspend any school in case of sickness or epidemics. Section 11.

6. It is made the duty of the General Superintendent and Trustees, promptly to remove, or report for removal, any and all persons connected with the public schools or academies known to be abolitionists, or who disseminate, or attempt to disseminate, directly or indirectly, abolition doctrines, or any other fanatical sentiments, which, in their opinion, are dangerous to the peace and safety of the Choctaw people. Section 13.

By a separate act, the Board of Trustees was authorized to propose to the Missionary Boards, having schools under contract with the Nation, the insertion of a clause providing for a termination of the contract by either party on giving six months' notice.

With respect to the question, "Shall we submit to the provisions and restrictions imposed by this new legislation, as a condition of continued connection with the national schools?" the views of the Prudential Committee and the brethren of the mission have been entirely in declared agreement. As stated in the last Annual Report to the Board, (p. 166,) "the Committee decided at once that they could not carry on the schools upon the new basis; and in the propriety of this action the missionaries concur." The concurrence of the missionaries in this view, viz., that they could not carry on the schools with a change from the original basis to that of the new law, may be seen clearly expressed in their correspondence with the Secretary having charge of the Indian missions; particularly in the following communications: From Messrs. Kingsbury and Byington, as the committee of the mission, under dates of December 14 and 27, 1853; Mr. Kingsbury, January 4, and April 25, 1854; Mr. C. C. Copeland, March 1, 1854; Mr. Stark, August 22, 1854; Mr. Edwards, July 13, 1854; Mr. H. K. Copeland, May 16, 1854. See also letters from Mr. Chamberlain, January 7, and June

20, 1854. In some of these, the declaration is made, that, in the apprehension of the writers, the schools must be relinquished, *if the law should not be repealed;* one specifying, as justificatory reasons, the breach of contract made, and the increased difficulty of obtaining teachers—reasons also assigned by others; another stating that he "never could consent to take charge of a school under such regulations;" a third testifying, not only for himself, but for every other member of the mission, an unwillingness to continue connection with the schools with subjection to the new requirements; a fourth affirming his "feeling" to be "that a strong remonstrance should be presented to the Council, and on the strength of it let the mission lay down these schools;" which, he states, would not involve "giving up the instruction of these children, but would be simply changing the plan," inasmuch as, according to his and others' understanding of the case, the new law not having application to other than the national schools, "at every station it will be found an easy matter to have as large, and in some cases even larger, than our present boarding schools."

In certain other communications, the view which the Committee adopted, is exhibited, together with the opinion that it would be better to wait for a movement on the part of the Choctaw authorities before giving up the schools. See letters from Mr. Byington, December 26, 1853; January 3 and 12, April 15, 1854; Mr. Kingsbury, February 1 and 21, 1854; Mr. Chamberlain, January 13, 1854; Mr. Stark, February 6, 1854. This view was also formally announced, as understood by the Committee, in resolutions of the mission at its meeting in May, 1854, embracing a recommendation of a course of procedure with the hope of securing the repeal by the next Council of the obnoxious law. See Minutes, and letters of Mr. C. C. Copeland, May 19, and June 9, 1854. The Prudential Committee, in the exercise of their discretion, as a principal party to the contract, preferred another method, viz., to address the Council directly, and sent a letter, under date of August 1, 1854, to one of the missionaries for presentation. The missionary, with the advice of his brethren given at their meeting in September, (intelligence of which was received at the Missionary House, October 20, thirty-five days subsequent to the meeting of the Board at Hartford,) withheld the letter, on the ground that, in their judgment, its presentation would defeat the object at which it aimed, and be "disastrous to the churches, to the Choctaws, and to the best interests of the colored race." In respect to this action for obtaining the repeal of the school law, there was a difference between the mission and the Committee. The missionaries desired delay, and the leaving of the matter to their management. The decision of the Committee, approved by the Board, "not to conduct the boarding schools in the Choctaw Nation in conformity with the principles prescribed by the recent legislation of the Choctaw Council,"* was in agreement with the previously and subsequently expressed sentiments of all the missionaries; the objection felt by some of them to this resolution being, not to the position which it assumes, but to the declaration of it at that time by the Board. This being a determined question, its settlement formed no part of the object for which the Deputation was sent.

Two other questions, however, required careful examination; and on these free conference was had with the brethren at their stations, and in a meeting of the mission held at Good-water, April 25 and 26, Mr. Edwards, who was absent from the mission, and Dr. Hobbs, not being present: 1. The law remaining unrepealed, is it practicable to carry on the schools while refusing conformity to the new "conditions, limitations and restrictions" imposed by it? 2. If so, is it expedient to do it?

On the first of these questions, the opinion of the missionaries was in the affirmative. No attempt has been made to carry out these new provisions. The Trustees and General Superintendent have not given the required bond. One of the Trustees informed me that he should not give it, and that in his belief the law would remain a dead letter, if not repealed, as it was his hope that it would be. The course of the missionaries has been in no degree changed by it. The teaching of slaves

* Resolution of the Board adopted at Hartford.

in these schools has never been practiced or contemplated. The law was aimed at such teaching in their families and Sabbath schools. So the missionaries and the people understand it. It is generally known among the latter that the former are ready to give up these schools, rather than retain them on condition of subjection to this law. Our brethren are now carrying on the schools, and doing in all other respects, just as they were before the new law was enacted; and they have confidence that they may continue to do so.

The second question was one of more uncertainty to my own mind, and in the minds of some of the mission. The maintenance of these schools is a work of great difficulty. In the opinion of several of the missionaries, it was at least doubtful whether the cost in health, perplexity, trouble in obtaining teachers, time which might be devoted to preaching, and money, was not too great for the results; and it was suggested that an opportunity, afforded by divine Providence for relieving us from a burden too heavy to sustain for nine years longer, should be embraced. See letters from Mr. Hotchkin, March 21, 1854; Mr. H. K. Copeland, January 23, and July 27, 1854; Mr. Lansing, December 22, 1853, and May 13, 1854. The fact and manner of the suspension of the school at Goodwater, in 1853, were portentous of increasing embarrassment from other causes than the new school law; and grave objections exist to the connection with civil government of any department of missionary operations.

My observation of the schools, however, interested me much in their behalf. They are doing a good work for the nation. Many of the pupils become Christian wives, mothers and teachers. The people appreciate them highly; and I was assured of a general desire that they should remain in the hands of the mission, unsubjected to the inadmissible new conditions of the recent legislation. In view of all the relations, which after full consideration the subject seemed to have, the following resolution, expressing the sentiment of the Deputation and the mission, was cheerfully and unanimously adopted by the mission; one of the older members, however, avowing some difficulty in giving his assent to the latter part of it, viz:

"*Resolved,* That while we should esteem it our duty to relinquish the female boarding schools at Pine Ridge, Wheelock and Stockbridge, rather than to carry them on under the provisions and restrictions of the late school law, yet regarding it as improbable that the requirement so to do will be enforced, we deem it important, in the present circumstances of the Choctaw Nation and mission, to continue our connection with them *on the original basis,* and carry them forward with new hope and energy."

Our hope of being allowed to maintain these schools as heretofore, and make them increasingly useful, may be disappointed. Neither the Prudential Committee nor the mission wish to retain them, if they for whose benefit alone they have been taken, prefer that we should give them up. The relinquishment of them would be a release from a weight of labor, anxiety and care, that nothing but our love for the Choctaws could induce us longer to bear. Our desire is only to do them good.

A second subject of conference, but the one first considered, was the principles, particularly in relation to slavery, on which the Prudential Committee, with the formally expressed approbation of the Board, aim to conduct its missions. I found certain misapprehensions existing in the minds of a portion of the mission in regard to the origin and circumstances of the action of the Board at the last annual meeting, which I was happy to correct. Several of the members, including one of the two not present at this meeting of the mission, have ever cordially approved the correspondence in which the views of principles entertained by the Committee were stated. Others, being with those just referred to a decided majority of the whole body as at present constituted, have expressed their agreement with those views as freely explained in personal intercourse, with an exhibition of the intended meaning of his own written language, by the Secretary who was the organ of the Committee in communicating them. Others have supposed themselves to differ, in some degree, from these principles when correctly apprehended. A full comparison of views, to their mutual great satisfaction, showed much less difference than was thought to exist between the members of the mission themselves, and between a part of the mission and what the Deputation understands to be the views of the Prudential Committee. A statement of principles drawn up at Good-water, as being in the estimation of the Deputation (distinctly and repeatedly so declared) those which the Committee had set forth in their correspondence, particularly that had with the mission in 1848, was unanimously adopted, as the brethren say, "for the better and more harmonious prosecution of the great objects of the Choctaw mission on the part of the Prudential Committee and the members of the mission, and for the removal of any and all existing difficulties which have grown out of public discussions and action on the subject of slavery; it being understood that the sentiments now approved are not in the estimation of the brethren of the mission new, but such as for a long series of years have really been held by them."

The statement is given, with the appended resolution, in the following words:

1. Slavery, as a system, and in its own proper nature, is what it is described to be, in the General Assembly's Act of 1818, and the Report of the American Board adopted at Brooklyn in 1845.

2. Privation of liberty in holding slaves is, therefore, not to be ranked with things indifferent, but with those which, if not made right by special justificatory circumstances and the intention of the doer, are morally wrong.

3. Those are to be admitted to the communion of the church, of whom the missionary and (in Presbyterian churches) his session have satisfactory evidence that they are in fellowship with Christ.

4. The evidence, in one view of it, of fellowship with Christ, is a manifested desire and aim to be conformed, in all things, to the spirit and requirements of the word of God.

5. Such desire and aim are to be looked for in reference to slavery, slaveholding, and dealing with slaves, as in regard to other matters; not less, not more.

6. The missionary must, under a solemn sense of responsibility to Christ, act on his own judgment of that evidence when obtained, and on the manner of obtaining it. He is at liberty to pursue that course which he may deem most discreet in eliciting views and feelings as to slavery, as with respect to other things, right views and feelings concerning which he seeks as evidence of Christian character.

7. The missionary is responsible, not for correct views and action on the part of his session and church members, but only for an honest and proper endeavor to secure correctness of views and action under the same obligations and limitations on this subject as on others. He is to go only to the extent of his rights and responsibilities as a minister of Christ.

8. The missionary, in the exercise of a wise discretion as to time, place, manner and amount of instruction, is decidedly to discountenance indulgence in known sin and the neglect of known duty, and so to instruct his hearers that they may understand all Christian duty. With that wisdom which is profitable to direct, he is to exhibit the legitimate bearing of the gospel upon every moral evil, in order to its removal in the most desirable way; and upon slavery, as upon other moral evils. As a missionary, he has nothing to do with political questions and agitations. He is to deal alone, and as a Christian instructor and pastor, with what is morally wrong, that the people of God may separate themselves therefrom, and a right standard of moral action be held up before the world.

9. While, as in war, there can be no shedding of blood without sin somewhere attached, and yet the individual soldier may not be guilty of it; so, while slavery is always sinful, we cannot esteem every one who is legally a slaveholder a wrongdoer for sustaining the legal relation. When it is made unavoidable by the laws of the State, the obligations of guardianship, or the demands of humanity, it is not to be deemed an offence against the rule of Christian right. Yet missionaries are carefully to guard, and in the proper way to warn others to guard, against unduly extending this plea of necessity or the good of the slave, against making it a cover for the love and

practice of slavery, or a pretence for not using efforts that are lawful and practicable to extinguish this evil.

10. Missionaries are to enjoin upon all masters and servants obedience to the directions specially addressed to them in the Holy Scriptures, and to explain and illustrate the precepts containing them.

11. In the exercise of discipline in the churches, under the same obligations and limitations as in regard to other acts of wrong-doing, and which are recognized in the action of ministers with reference to other matters in evangelical churches where slavery does not exist, missionaries are to set their faces against all overt acts in relation to this subject, which are manifestly unchristian and sinful; such as the treatment of slaves with inhumanity and oppression; keeping from them the knowledge of God's holy will; disregarding the sanctity of the marriage relation; trifling with the affections of parents, and setting at naught the claims of children on their natural protectors; and regarding and treating human beings as articles of merchandise.

12. For various reasons, we agree in the inexpediency of our employing slave labor in other cases than those of manifest necessity; it being understood that the objection of the Prudential Committee to the employment of such labor is to that extent only.

13. Agreeing thus in essential principles, missionaries associated in the same field should exercise charity towards each other, and have confidence in one another, in respect to differences which, from diversity of judgment, temperament, or other individual peculiarities, and from difference of circumstances in which they are placed, may arise among them in the practical carrying out of these principles; and we think that this should be done by others towards us as a missionary body.

Resolved, That we agree in the foregoing as an expression of our views concerning our relations and duties as missionaries in regard to the subject treated of; and are happy to believe that, having this agreement with what we now understand to be the views of the Prudential Committee, we may have their confidence, as they have ours, in the continued prosecution together of the great work to which the great Head of the church has called us among this people.

The statement thus approved was read throughout, and was afterwards considered in detail, each member of the mission expressing his views upon it as fully, and keeping it under consideration as long, as he desired to do. After the assent given to it, article by article, on the day following it was again read, and the question was taken upon it as a whole, with the appended resolution, each of the eight members giving his vote in favor of its adoption. It is perhaps proper also to mention that no change by way of emendation, addition or omission of phraseology was found necessary to make it such as any member of the mission would be willing to accept. It should farther be stated, that while the first article was under consideration, the act of the General Assembly of the Presbyterian church, adopted in 1818, was read, and its strongest expressions duly weighed. The document thus considered and referred to, is herewith submitted as a part of this report.*

---

* "The General Assembly of the Presbyterian Church, having taken into consideration the subject of slavery, think proper to make known their sentiments upon it to the churches and people under their care. We consider the voluntary enslaving of one part of the human race by another, as a gross violation of the most precious and sacred rights of human nature; as utterly inconsistent with the law of God, which requires us to love our neighbor as ourselves, and as totally irreconcilable with the spirit and principles of the gospel of Christ, which enjoins that 'all things whatsoever ye would that men should do to you, do ye even so to them.' Slavery creates a paradox in the moral system; it exhibits rational, accountable and immortal beings in such circumstances as scarcely to leave them the power of moral action. It exhibits them as dependent on the will of others, whether they shall receive religious instruction; whether they shall know and worship the true God; whether they shall enjoy the ordinances of the Gospel; whether they shall perform the duties and cherish the endearments of husbands and wives, parents and children, neighbors and friends; whether they shall preserve their chastity and purity, or regard the dictates of justice and humanity. Such are some of the consequences of slavery—consequences not imaginary, but which connect themselves with its very existence. The evils to which the slave is always exposed often take place in fact, and in their very worst degree and form; and where all of them do not take place, as we rejoice to say in many instances, through the influence of the principles of humanity and religion on the mind of masters, they do not—

So also was adduced the abundant testimony contained in the Report of the American Board adopted in 1845, as to what in its view slavery, without qualification of place or time, and as it exists in the United States and among the Indians, is: such as its classification of slavery with war, polygamy, the

---

still the slave is deprived of his natural right, degraded as a human being, and exposed to the danger of passing into the hands of a master who may inflict upon him all the hardships and injuries which inhumanity and avarice may suggest.

"From this view of the consequences resulting from the practice into which Christian people have most inconsistently fallen, of enslaving a portion of their brethren of mankind—for 'God hath made of one blood all nations of men to dwell on the face of the earth'—it is manifestly the duty of all Christians who enjoy the light of the present day, when the inconsistency of slavery, both with the dictates of humanity and religion, has been demonstrated, and is generally seen and acknowledged, to use their honest, earnest, and unwearied endeavors, to correct the errors of former times, and as speedily as possible to efface this blot on our holy religion, and to obtain the complete abolition of slavery throughout Christendom, and if possible throughout the world.

"We rejoice that the Church to which we belong commenced, as early as any other in this country, the good work of endeavoring to put an end to slavery, and that in the same work many of its members have ever since been, and now are, among the most active, vigorous and efficient laborers. We do, indeed, tenderly sympathize with those portions of our Church and our country where the evil of slavery has been entailed upon them; where a great, and the most virtuous part of the community abhor slavery, and wish its extermination as sincerely as any others—but where the number of slaves, their ignorance, and their vicious habits generally, render an immediate and universal emancipation inconsistent alike with the safety and happiness of the master and the slave. With those who are thus circumstanced, we repeat that we tenderly sympathize. At the same time we earnestly exhort them to continue, and if possible to increase their exertions to effect a total abolition of slavery. We exhort them to suffer no greater delay to take place in this most interesting concern, than a regard to the public welfare truly and indispensably demands.

"As our country has inflicted a most grievous injury on the unhappy Africans, by bringing them into slavery, we cannot indeed urge that we should add a second injury to the first, by emancipating them in such manner as that they will be likely to destroy themselves or others. But we do think, that our country ought to be governed in this matter by no other consideration than an honest and impartial regard to the happiness of the injured party, uninfluenced by the expense or inconvenience which such a regard may involve. We, therefore, warn all who belong to our denomination of Christians against unduly extending this plea of necessity; against

castes of India, and other things which it speaks of as "social and moral evils;" and such language as the following: "The Committee do not deem it necessary to discuss the general subject of slavery as it exists in these United States, or to enlarge on the wickedness of the system, or on the disastrous

---

making it a cover for the love and practice of slavery, or a pretence for not using efforts that are lawful and practicable, to extinguish this evil.

"And we, at the same time, exhort others to forbear harsh censures, and uncharitable reflections on their brethren, who unhappily live among slaves whom they cannot immediately set free; but who, at the same time, are really using all their influence, and all their endeavors, to bring them into a state of freedom, as soon as a door for it can be safely opened.

"Having thus expressed our views of slavery, and of the duty indispensably incumbent on all Christians to labor for its complete extinction, we proceed to recommend—and we do it with all the earnestness and solemnity which this momentous subject demands—a particular attention to the following points.

"We recommend to all our people to patronize and encourage the Society lately formed for colonizing in Africa, the land of their ancestors, the free people of color in our country. We hope that much good may result from the plans and efforts of this Society. And while we exceedingly rejoice to have witnessed its origin and organization among the holders of slaves, as giving an unequivocal pledge of their desires to deliver themselves and their country from the calamity of slavery; we hope that those portions of the American union, whose inhabitants are by a gracious Providence more favorably circumstanced, will cordially, and liberally, and earnestly co-operate with their brethren, in bringing about the great end contemplated.

"We recommend to all the members of our religious denomination, not only to permit, but to facilitate and encourage the instruction of their slaves in the principles and duties of the Christian religion; by granting them liberty to attend on the preaching of the gospel, when they have opportunity; by favoring the instruction of them in the Sabbath school, wherever those schools can be formed; and by giving them all other proper advantages for acquiring a knowledge of their duty both to God and to man. We are perfectly satisfied that it is incumbent on all Christians to communicate religious instruction to those who are under their authority; so that the doing of this in the case before us, so far from operating, as some have apprehended that it might, as an incitement to insubordination and insurrection, would, on the contrary, operate as the most powerful means for the prevention of those evils.

"We enjoin it on all church sessions and presbyteries, under the care of this Assembly, to discountenance, and as far as possible to prevent all cruelty of whatever kind in the treatment of slaves; especially the cruelty of separating husband and wife, parents and children, and that which con-

*

moral and social influences which slavery exerts upon the less enlightened and less civilized communities where the missionaries of this Board are laboring:" "The unrighteousness of the principles on which the whole system is based, and the violation of the natural rights of man, the debasement, wickedness and misery it involves, and which are in fact witnessed to a greater or less extent wherever it exists, must call forth the hearty condemnation of all possessed of Christian feeling and sense of right, and make its removal an object of earnest and prayerful desire to every friend of God and man:" "Strongly as your committee are convinced of the wrongfulness and evil tendencies of slaveholding, and ardently as they desire its speedy and universal termination, still they cannot think that in all cases it involves individual guilt in such a manner that every person implicated in it can, on scriptural grounds, be excluded from Christian fellowship. In the language of Dr. Chalmers, 'Distinction ought to be made between the character of a *system*, and the character of the persons whom circumstances have implicated therewith; nor would it always be just, if all the recoil and horror wherewith the former is contemplated, were visited in the form of condemnation and moral indignancy upon the latter. Slavery we hold to be a system chargeable with atrocities and evils, often the most hideous and appalling which have either afflicted or deformed our species; yet we must not, therefore, say of every man born within its territory, who has grown up familiar with its sickening spectacles, and not only by his habits been

sists in selling slaves to those who will either themselves deprive these unhappy people of the blessings of the gospel, or who will transport them to places where the gospel is not proclaimed, or where it is forbidden to slaves to attend upon its institutions. And if it shall ever happen that a Christian professor in our communion shall sell a slave who is also in communion and good standing with our church, contrary to his or her will and inclination, it ought immediately to claim the particular attention of the proper church judicature; and unless there be such peculiar circumstances attending the case as can but seldom happen, it ought to be followed, without delay, by a suspension of the offender from all the privileges of the church, till he repent, and make all the reparation in his power to the injured party." See Assembly's Digest, pp. 274–8.

inured to its transactions and sights, but who by inheritance is himself the owner of slaves, that unless he make the resolute sacrifice, and renounce his property in slaves, he is, therefore, not a Christian, and should be treated as an outcast from all the distinctions and privileges of Christian society.'" And the language (quoted approvingly) unanimously uttered by the General Assembly of the Free Church of Scotland: "Without being prepared to adopt the principle that, in the circumstances in which they are placed, the churches in America ought to consider slaveholding *per se* an insuperable barrier in the way of enjoying Christian privileges, or an offence to be visited with excommunication, all must agree in holding that whatever rights the civil law of the land may give a master over his slaves as *chattels personal*, it cannot be but sin of the deepest dye to regard and treat them as such; and whosoever commits that sin in any sense, or deals otherwise than as a Christian man ought to deal with his fellow-man, whatever power the law may give him over them, ought to be held disqualified for Christian communion. Farther, it must be the opinion of all, that it is the duty of Christians, when they find themselves unhappily in the predicament of slaveholders, to aim, as far as it may be practicable, at the manumission of their slaves; and when that cannot be accomplished, to secure them in the enjoyment of the domestic relations, and of the means of religious training and education."

All this, and more, was immediately before the minds of the members of the mission, and with so much of the connection as to give the true sense, when they declared that slavery is what, in the documents referred to, it is described to be, and made their own the statement of principles above given, as those on which, as missionaries, they should deal with this subject in the circumstances of their field of labor, and when it is to them a practical missionary question.

The Cherokee mission in session at Park Hill, May 9, adopted a resolution of concurrence with the Choctaw mission in approving this statement.

Excluding two churches then connected with the mission of the Board, and since transferred to another mission, there were in 1848, under the care of the American Board, in the Choctaw Nation, six churches with a total membership of 536 persons, of whom 25 were slaveholders, and 64 were slaves. The churches are now 11 in number, containing 1,094 members; of whom, as nearly as I could ascertain, 20 are slaveholders, (some of them being husband and wife, and generally having but one or two slaves each,) and 60 are slaves. Six of the churches have no slaveholder in them; two have but one each. Of the slaveholders in these churches, four have been admitted since 1848; one by transfer from another denomination, and three on profession of their faith; none of the latter having been received since 1850. Statements were made to me respecting each of these latter cases, which show that the principles assented to by the mission at Good-water, as above presented, were practically carried out in regard to them.

In the Cherokee mission, in 1848, there were five churches, having 237 members, of whom 24 were slaveholders, and 23 were slaves. In the five churches now in that mission, there are 207 members, of whom 17 (there is uncertainty in regard to one of this number) are reported as slaveholders. Three have been admitted since 1848 on profession of their faith, and two by letter; one of the latter from a church in New Hampshire. Of these the same remark may be made as above in respect to similar cases among the Choctaws.

The Choctaw mission embraces eleven families and three large boarding schools. Five slaves, hired at their own desire, are in the employment of the missionaries. A less number are employed in the Cherokee mission. Gladly would the missionaries dispense with these, could the necessary amount of free labor for domestic service be obtained. Those who employ this slave labor, allege that it is to them a matter of painful necessity. They are known to resort to it unwillingly, and are not regarded as thereby giving their sanction to slavery. Some thus employed have been brought to a saving knowledge of divine truth.

The sentiments of these two missions as to the moral character of slavery, and the principles on which they should act with regard to it, are frankly and unequivocally avowed.

We are bound to believe them honest in the expression of these sentiments. It is their expectation that the principles thus acknowledged as their own will be those on which the missions will be conducted. The adjudication of particular cases must be left to the missionary. That it be so left, is his right; it is also unavoidable. The position of the missionaries is one of great difficulty, and should be appreciated. That there is such a diversity of judgment among them as men of independent thought and differing mental characteristics, who agree in essential principles, everywhere evince; and that they have, through a use of phraseology leading sometimes to a mutual misunderstanding of each other's views, supposed themselves to differ more widely than, in our conferences, they found themselves really to do, has been intimated. That none of them have sympathy with slavery; that, on the other hand, their influence is directly and strongly adverse to its continuance, while they are doing much in mitigation of its evils and to bless both master and slave, in the judgment of the Deputation, is beyond a doubt. By many they are denounced as abolitionists. Some of their slave-holding church members have left their churches for another connection on this account. Others have disconnected themselves from a system which they have learned to dislike and disapprove. Strong in the confidence and affection of many for whose salvation they have toiled and suffered, by the supporters of slavery, in and out of the nations, they undoubtedly are looked upon with growing suspicion. Surely we should not be willing needlessly to embarrass them in their blessed work. They are worthy of the confidence and warmest sympathy of every friend of the red man and of the black man. God is with them. In the Cherokee mission, the dispensation of his grace is not, indeed, now as in times past; and we have some seriousness of apprehension in regard to the progress of the gospel among that people. Still the divine presence is not wanting. Among the Choctaws rapid advance is making. Converts are multiplying; the fruits of the gospel abound. Both missions need reinforcement. Men filled with the spirit of Christ, able to endure hardness, of practical wisdom, which knows how to do good, and not to do only harm when good is meant, men of faith, energy, meekness and prayer, who will commend themselves to every man's conscience in the sight of God as his servants, are required. It gave me pleasure to assure the missions of the strong desire of the Prudential Committee, and of my future personal endeavors, to obtain such men for them. No philanthropist can behold the change which has been wrought for these lately pagan, savage tribes, now orderly christianized communities, advancing in civilization, to take ere long, if they go on in their course, their place with those whose Christian civilization is the growth of many centuries, without admiration and delight. But there is much yet to be done for them. "This nation," says the Choctaw mission in a published letter, "in its improvements, schools, churches, and public spirit pertaining to the great cause of benevolence, is but an *infant*." We must not expect too much from these churches in which we glory. Much fostering and training do they yet need; and there are many souls yet to be enlightened and saved. Wonderful as are the renovation and elevation which the gospel, taught in its simplicity by faithful men, has already given to these communities, our only hope for them, and for the colored race in the midst of them, is in the continued application of the same power through the same instrumentality.

It was the privilege of the Deputation to spend a part of three days, including a Sabbath, at Spencer Academy, an institution containing one hundred male pupils, excellently managed under the charge of the Board of the General Assembly; and to attend there a "big meeting," or a camp meeting, at which several hundreds were present. My intercourse with brethren at that station, and the scenes in which I there mingled; the fellowship in Christ with the heralds of his cross, some of them bowed with the weight of many years of wearing toil and affliction, and hastening to their glorious crown already won by honored names, no longer with them, of our own mission; and the interchange of sympathy with the disciples of Christ, whom God has given them as the fruit of their labor, will ever live among the pleasantest recollections of my life. I am constrained to repeat my testimony to the fraternal and Christian spirit with which the brethren met my endeavors to remove difficulties, strengthen the ties that bind them and the Board together, and clear the way for harmonious and more energetic prosecution of the great work in which we are associated. To a good degree this object, we may hope, has been gained. To Him, whose is their work and ours, and to whom the interests involved are infinitely more precious than to any of us who are connected with them, we commit the future keeping of this great trust.

It is due to the Choctaw mission that I communicate to the Committee the following resolution, presented by the Rev. Mr. Byington, and adopted by the mission at the close of its meeting at Good-water:

"*Resolved,* That the cordial thanks of the members of the mission be presented to the Rev. Geo. W. Wood, the Secretary of the A. B. C. F. M., who is with us as a Deputation from the Prudential Committee, for his kind, wise and successful efforts in our mission to remove the weight of anxiety which has long pressed down our hearts in connection with the subject of slavery. We now rejoice much in this mutual and kind interchange of thoughts and affections. We would pray for grace ever to walk in the path of life, and that blessings may attend him, while with us and on his way home, his family and brethren during his absence, as well as our mission and the American Board and all its officers. With peculiar sincerity of heart and gratitude to our Savior, we present to him this token of regard for our dear brother, and make this record of divine mercy toward our mission."

All which is respectfully submitted,

GEO. W. WOOD.

Rooms of the A. B. C. F. M., New York, June 13, 1855.

This communication of the Prudential Committee was referred to a special committee, consisting of Dr. Beman, Dr. Thomas De Witt, Dr. Hawes, Chief Justice Williams, Doct. Lyndon A. Smith, Dr, J. A. Stearns, and Hon. Linus Child, who subsequently made the following report:

Your committee have endeavored to look at this paper in its intrinsic character and practical bearings, and they are happy

to state their unanimous conviction, that this visit will mark an auspicious era in the history of these missions. The report of Mr. Wood is characterized by great clearness and precision; and it presents the whole matters pending between the Prudential Committee and these missions fully before us. The conferences of the Deputation with the missionaries appear to have been conducted in a truly Christian spirit; and the results which are set forth in the resolutions, adopted with much deliberation and after full discussion, are such as we may all hail with Christian gratitude.

It is the opinion of your committee that the great end which has been aimed at by the Prudential Committee in their correspondence with these missions, for several years past, and by the Board in their resolutions adopted at the last annual meeting, has been substantially accomplished. While your committee admit that there may be some incidental points on which an honest diversity of opinion may exist, yet they fully believe that this adjustment should be deemed satisfactory, and that farther agitation is not called for. While your committee cannot take it upon themselves to predict what new developments, calling for new action hereafter, *may* take place, they are unanimously of the opinion that the Prudential Committee, and these laborious and efficient missionaries on this field of Christian effort, may go forward, on the basis adopted, in perfect harmony in the prosecution of their future work.

Your committee feel that the thanks of this Board are due to Mr. Wood and our missionary brethren, for the manner in which they have met, considered, and adjusted these difficult matters which have long been in debate; and at the same time they would not forget that God is the source of all true light in our deepest darkness, and that to him *all the glory is ever due.*

The foregoing report of the select committee was adopted by the Board.

www.ingramcontent.com/pod-product-compliance
Lightning Source LLC
LaVergne TN
LVHW011144110826
845150LV00008B/2507
9781418192082